MW00981779

JAYS

BACKYARD BIRDS

Lynn Stone

The Rourke Corporation, Inc.
Vero Beach, Florida 32964

PHOTO CREDITS
© Tom Vezo: cover, pages 7, 8, 13, 17; © Lynn M. Stone: title page, pages 4, 10, 12; page 15 courtesy of Duncraft, Concord, NH; © Tom J. Ulrich: pages 18, 21

COVER ART:
James Spence

EDITORIAL SERVICES:
Penworthy Learning Systems

Library of Congress Cataloging-in-Publication Data

Stone, Lynn M.
    Jays / by Lynn M. Stone.
        p. cm. — (Backyard birds)
    Includes index
    Summary: Describes the physical characteristics, habitats, and behavior of different kinds of jays, including the blue jay, Steller's jay, and gray jay.
    ISBN 0-86593-473-8
    1. Jays—Juvenile literature. [1. Jays.] I. Title II. Series.
Stone, Lynn M. Backyard birds.
QL696.P2367S76 1998
598.8'64—dc21   98–2727
                                                               CIP
                                                                AC

Printed in the USA

TABLE OF CONTENTS

JAYS

Jays are big, noisy perching birds. Most **species** (SPEE sheez), or kinds, of jays are very colorful.

Like us, jays are **omnivores** (AHM nuh VAWRZ). That means they eat both plant and animal matter.

Jays are often seen in backyard trees, bushes, and birdfeeders. They love handouts. Some of them—Steller's jays and gray jays, for example— are beggars at campsites, too.

Scrub jays become quite tame. They will take peanuts and other treats from the hand!

Bold and beautiful, this scrub jay perches on a photographer's hand. For its trust, the jay will get a peanut.

WHAT JAYS LOOK LIKE

North American jays are usually blue with some black and white. Even the green jay has a blue cap. The gray and brown jays, though, have no blue feathers.

Most jays are between 9 and 11 inches (23 and 28 centimeters) long, but the brown jay is bigger.

The blue jay and the dark Steller's jay have crests. The other six species of jays in the United States and Canada do not.

Best known of the jays is the blue jay.

WHERE JAYS LIVE

Jays live all over the United States and much of Canada. The blue jay has a wide **range** (RAYNJ), or living area, in the East and West. The Steller's jay lives in and west of the Rocky Mountains. The gray jay lives in Canada and the northern United States.

The piñyon and scrub jays are found in the West. Scrub jays also live in Florida.

The ranges of the green, brown, and gray-breasted jays are in Mexico.

A green jay inspects an orange in a backyard.

THE JAY FAMILY

The eight species of jays in Canada and the United States are cousins of magpies, crows, ravens, and nutcrackers. (Another 11 species of jays live in Mexico.)

All of these birds are omnivores. They have rounded wings, long tails, and loud calls.

The largest bird in the family is the raven. It looks like a super-sized crow. A raven may be 21 inches (53 centimeters) long.

Most ravens and crows are not as tame as jays. In winter, though, they sometimes visit backyards for food scraps.

A Clark's nutcracker, here on a rock in the Colorado mountains, is in the jay family.

On the lookout for scraps, a Steller's jay perches on a campground stump.

The gray-breasted jay is a Mexican species that lives in a small part of the United States.

JAYS IN THE BACKYARD

Like other birds, jays need food, water, and a place to perch. Backyards with food, water, and trees will draw jays from nearby woodlands.

With a birdbath, you can provide water for jays and other birds. A heated birdbath will give them open water even in winter.

Not everyone likes these good-looking birds in the yard. Jays may scare other birds away from feeders.

Sunflower seeds on a birdfeeder look good to a hungry blue jay.

BACKYARD FOOD FOR JAYS

Jays are most likely to use birdfeeders in winter. Jays are quick to find new feeders and help themselves to sunflower seeds, **suet** (SOO it), nutmeats, cracked corn, berries, and peanuts.

Blue jays do not like feeders that swing. They need a steady perch, and they often feed on the ground.

Scrub jays and blue jays love peanuts. Steller's jays eat sunflower seeds, nutmeats, peanuts, and fruit.

Gray jays like to sample almost any food at feeders and camps.

A blue jay hops among sunflower seeds under a backyard birdfeeder.

JAY HABITS

Blue jays are beautiful and bold. In noisy flocks they sometimes dive-bomb cats, squirrels, owls, and hawks. Scientists call this behavior **mobbing** (MAHB ing).

Mobbing jays don't hurt their targets. Jays do, however, often confuse and frighten the animals they mob.

Sometimes smaller birds chase and dive-bomb blue jays! The small birds seem to sense that jays might eat their eggs or even their babies.

The gray jay's bold habits have earned it nicknames such as camp robber and grease bird.

JAY NESTS

Jays build nests of sticks in trees. For jays, neatness does not count.

Blue jay nests are usually more than 10 feet (3 meters) above ground. Blue jays often nest in evergreen trees, like spruces or pines.

Scrub jays are very **social** (SO shul) birds. They like each other's company. Pairs of scrub jays build their nests close to one another. These little bird villages are called **colonies** (KAHL uh neez).

A mother blue jay tries to settle down on her babies to warm them.

BABY JAYS

A mother jay lays two to seven eggs. Her eggs are called a **clutch** (KLUCH). Most jay clutches have four eggs.

Jays sit on their eggs to keep them warm. Jays **incubate** (IN kyuh BAYT) for about 17 days.

Baby jays take about 18 days to grow before they can fly. During that time, the babies are fed by the parents at the nest.

Glossary

clutch (KLUCH) — two or more jay's eggs in a nest

colonies (KAHL uh neez) — places where groups of birds of the same kind nest close to each other; the birds group themselves

incubate (IN kyuh BAYT) — to keep eggs warm until they hatch

mobbing (MAHB ing) — the bothering of a bird or animal by a flock of birds of another kind

omnivore (AHM nuh VAWR) — an animal that eats both plant and animal matter

range (RAYNJ) — the entire area over which a plant or animal might be found in its natural environment

social (SO shul) — liking the company of others

species (SPEE sheez) — within a group of closely related animals, one certain kind, such as a *blue* jay

suet (SOO it) — hardened animal fat

INDEX

FURTHER READING:

Find out more about Backyard Birds with these helpful books and information sites:
• Burnie, David. *Bird*. Knopf, 1988
• Mahnken, Jan. *The Backyard Bird-Lover's Guide.* Storey Communications, 1996
• Parsons, Alexandra. *Amazing Birds*. Knopf, 1990
• *Field Guide to the Birds of North America*. National Geographic, 1983
• Cornell Laboratory of Ornithology online at http://birdsource.cornell.edu
• National Audubon Society online at www.audubon.org